I'M HERE TO FIND OUT

HOW TO LEAVE WITH THE SELF

AHSAHTA PRESS
BOISE, IDAHO
2015

THE NEW SERIES

#69

THIS IS THE HOMELAND

MARY HICKMAN

Ahsahta Press, Boise State University, Boise, Idaho 83725-1525
ahsahtapress.org
Cover design by Quemadura / Book design by Janet Holmes

LIBRARY OF CONGRESS CATALOGING-IN-PUBLICATION DATA

Hickman, Mary, 1979–
[Poems. Selections]
This is the homeland / Mary Hickman.
pages cm.—(The new series ; #69)
ISBN 978-1-934103-61-6 (pbk. : alk. paper)—ISBN 1-934103-61-6 (pbk. : alk. paper)
I. Title.
PS3608.I2755A6 2015
811'.6—DC23
2014049979

Acknowledgments appear on page 65.

For Kirsten Just

CONTENTS

Ungirdled, she came forward. And blessed the awaking throat and shaking head. And blessed the hair the oak.

This is the genuine christine body and blood, shut your eyes. White teeth. Will you? Skip gravely about. Legs, the loose folds of gown, the plump patron of lips.

The mockery of it! Her absurd name and neck. My name is absurd too.

My name for her is best: the sea! I must teach her. Come look over the water. Harbourmouth mother. Eyesfromthesea mother. Curled lips a lovely. Murmured loveliest of them all. A white bowl holding the sluggish sea.

That fellow I was in the radiant sea! Curling, laughed, white glittering teeth.

Sea pulses veil my sight. The sea wants morning. Whitewave, wedded
words shimmering on the dim tide. A cloud in deeper green, a bowl of
bitter water. Song: I sang it alone in the house. For those words.

> Her secrets: her glass of water filled while
> all prayed on their knees: *iubilantium te
> virginum chorus excipiat*. Mother, let me
> be and let me live, for Chrissake.

The blessings of God, the bag, the damned eggs. You make strong tea.
Do you pray, Mary? Do you then suddenly vigorously care?

Come. Get an elbow, a lovely morning, glory to God, old and secret.
Heart of my heart, laid at your feet, I'm stony. Today bards must drink.
This day will do his duty. I have to swim, the unclean bard washed by
the Gulf Stream, a slice of you.

Right hand came down into the bowl. So warm. The sea. So thick with salt.

> The weight of the body cracking. Law of falling bodies. They all fall to the ground.

> What is home?

A flower I think. A yellow flower with flattened petals.

Language of flowers. Narcotic. O Mairy. Could you make a thing like that? Lovely water cool out of a well. Stone cold hole. Goblet a silence a white flutter then all sank. He foresaw his body naked in the womb, bud of flesh: limp languid floating flower.

Two birds with one head walking on mirthfully—O
night in the hall when to lift skirts to step over you as
you lay in your most innocent moment. My will: his
will that fronts me.

Here I watched the birds go, they came, I flew. Easily
flew with clown's awe. Look upon you, lust after you.
Thou art the gateway under me still. Speak!

Frail plumes and in a flaw of softness—an altar and let
our crooked smokes climb from our bless'd altar: breast
and pointed red. Post yourself into the box, Mary.
Yellow heaven—slim fingers of the red flower—*sua
voce*—.

A flock, small white going slowly down the wind. Clouds, ankles, stubble of the fields at play in the quiet evening. Walked calmly and read. Walking and reading. What's the best news? Home. Gay sweet chirping within. Put in the book fields, ankles, stubble. Did you try? Poured from the kettle into a bowl, yellow into our father who art in heaven. Yellow bowl in pink tissue—you. And the damage? A girl. Slim fingers reckon the fruit.

Come tonight blushing, tiptoeing nearer heaven and cover the noise . . .
Is it not faithful? An inward light first hiding, a runaway in blighted
body. Sweet cinnamon leaves all bare and forgiven her.

The comets laugh. I'll tell you, the damn comets cross; they know. The lord was there and there was music and I sang but broke out in a wheezing laugh and we did ample justice. I was with wife. I had bumped against hell. He held his caved hands. I was moulded. He shut his eyes tight, his body shrinking and blew a sweet chirp and was, by god, lost.

I don't want my name. He has hidden his own fair name
in a clown, in the dark corners of my crown my feet my
handkerchief. Your name is strange: Lapwing. You flew.
Seabedabbled lapwing, because you know.

I am anticipating what you have to say. I am asking
too much, tired of my voice. Lapwing. The voice that
makes love to the seacoast. Or his last written words.

You are a delusion. You, brought all this way, do you
believe?

Write! Visit! Help me believe. I called on the birds. This
will end. I shall be there, laughing into a shattering
daylight.

And scribble nightly, unwed.

REMEMBERING ANIMALS

1

On this couch,
goose liver–colored pillow
placed in my lap, I paint
the way. Touch my
gray neck
and you will find—

2

She had her scars done.

I'd like to think
I could solve the problems of
love lives, libraries, wildlife,
obfuscating
griefs.

3

In that story I told you,
I was locked in a room.

I would like to be offered
fresh white socks, in morning sun,
just as the taxi comes.

4

I kept thinking my
"hello"
would split.

Folding your limbs,
one through the other.

5

I see an animal
and I paint it.

Tenderness compels
the worst of us and
"who among us"
to watch as it enters that room called
rising.

6

I want to dream
just this just
a private rising
towards an otherwise
animal refrain.

TERRITORY

I

Blue flesh smokes up & quickly sucked
it out. The gorgeous view returned. The fertile

red valleys warming up. This is the way to the steel table.
This is the homeland.

II

Rub it all over the forearms   whitepush then red.
Sandalwood explains the crane nested in the mountain.
Her wild hips, jagged beak.

Body lumps & chest-hole. What land is this?

III

I was ironing my body so scrubbed

my forearms clean for holding
at least one heart a day.
Sometimes touching a lung or toes very dead
look burnt, the taste like
charred rice fields. Won't

retch won't retch retch.
Pick a prettier country.

IV

They have beautiful graves. I knelt in his chest. The lungs in
shreds. I pushed
the ribs back from my knees
—an offering.

V

        Twelve hours his chest
cracked &
died.
 (This is the way to the Azure.)
Care I what no did not know him. I know
better. At least
I know what.

I get so sick of their fat sternums.
Why save 'em? We are unsure.
See this brain box—which box are we in?

VI

With my hips to the shore, even 'em far, the Chinese shore.

REMEMBERING ANIMALS

1

It's hard to light
a photo shot
in torrential rain.

2

Today I don't
need girls to smell
of anything, but the snap
of leather
is a clap of midnight
or crack
of New Year's.

3

You know
I'd still love
to live in Spain.

Because of my bad headaches because of my glands my devotion
because with your image wandering in & out. A bowing figure is a
figure led home. Inhaled.

I'm led from my head to my hasty heels. Lying. Just

a gate. Should it rain
uncover your head to the river, she says.
Had your heart been decorated
with grasses. Had your bean-aphid heart been handed to me,
your ancestral heart the size of an endive & bent.

If you may be taken with a heel—
I was indecently treated & changed, she said
Look at my skin how it attacks,
Right, its larva & above
A good breath from the navel

Held in half with your vent
Dusted lung: Unfold to pray

Pushed from onionskin
Bent at the body & cracked Eleusinian:
Silk me this shell, cloth pulled
From bone, from awe & turned away

GEESE RISING

Bring my middle to ∨ isosceles where I become bees acting like geese's
wings really pins

And lock my waist into sky (arias!) and more silver, really chalk, that
charts

Birds ascending in a ∨ of voice where I strive to be at perfect rights
with their aerial beaks

If you will carry me, she says
If you will carry me, the geese repeat
And you should echo

SPINAL TWIST

Having arrived at the position to turn away
you know nothing in the spine hears the spine, its velvet cups
squeezed between bone.
Your wax wings pinned to one side, nailed
to the mat. Sluggish fat & rise. Front to go back.
60° she says. Collapse
the heart.
Between the mat and hand. Her imposter palms
& give your nerves a hearty pull. Hzzzt.
A sound in the neck, the rack.

MATADOR

My love, your palms are palms of Mexico mostly. Ringed or jointed.
Up! Up! Blushing to the elbow. Press your foot to your foot your knee.

      Belly belly belly ah bellyful of ginger &

a shock of red in the guts. My head in your lap. Up!

Then to simmer in orange to repot
yourself in silt in wreck in the power
of God. Because we speak of gardens, & lunge.

WOODCHOPPER

A word of warning for people with bad hearts:
If you are very stiff
skipping to hell your feet apart
If you have abdominal fat
& thighs
thighs! you'll grow old you'll grow
pink in a position we can't expect
& force your habit at the waist.

Thumb held straight, your other fingers make
a spire. With one hand nothing's held
captive. With both hands, advancing,
open the gates, see into pines.

In the thicket of divaricated thighs
send us Universal Esteem.
Bright thighfruit raised & alternate the bounty
of increase. My desire immense
domestic, she says. The words within her shell:
elk, yak, snout & crawler. Release your glands
to air. Your floating kidney to
ripe wheat. Then be tipped on your side,
                                        jiggered.

       Being made in the crotch of a bean plant with a net of nicotine
I imagine her knees pop.
She pulls threads from the air. Expiring. Latches to stems in the water.
She's rubbing her legs in steam.
Her noisy head in haze. Golden Foot Raised.

       Brows of kites of cumin borrowed from her milky braids your
pure-chirping vacuum voice. I sing a crying shame

       your body coral blue, been stripped
from earth's O

        Happy inert fan
my feet make—your breast a

mat you offer—stretch my seven-rhythm breath
—per what's electric—a bowstring row of bees—

Carve your wooden cheek in beams—

Youthful claps: luster [[]] sheen [[]] patina [[]] gleam [[]]

REMEMBERING ANIMALS

I

It's like recovering
a horse from a sale.

How it feels
to lengthen, all neck. Spine
to strengthen.

2

Replanting meadow,
I listen to a Saturday track
waiting for Sunday.

3

I paint animals,
necks stretched,
heads thrown back.

I think in this one the mane
drips a black like cartographer's ink.

I

Because he was so foreign, I bought a pretty boy with hooks & fists. His species sprouted pepper branches. Cities brought their split to heal.

    Spine-pointed bloom, sheath-white-William.
His cheek. A bridge. Ha, the stems of a bridge. To be famous & quick I cut it down. I cut it that morning & a tell-tale flush.
    He's god's r in pure sensation. Peeled his joints from the sand, knelt down to plant. In oil, in soil.

II

Pigeon-breasted boy, I could flower
to the end of May. A foot mislaid the holes & pebbles of the beach.
Birds covered over the gardens
with dull red glass. We pray.
I'll flay him alive. His graceful palms embedded. My white greekly
perfect. Hot webs
        to touch a thing like this—wild-sweet-William buds
early. Studied prayer, hone
the gay birdsong
                        we begin to hear respired hums.
A peep of white touches the spot. William.
Clean clean bloom along the head.

III

      I grew his strap-shaped image in the tub.   Knobs—discs—
cups sprung & cultivated a horn from the wreck of rib. I lashed
the Sweet Bough to his head,   Wealthy William.
He hauls a reef of skirt. William who lives.
His brain cries out in plenty. In habit. My fingers taper oval to hold
a pigeon's song of his. Drunk, what I said about the bud of ordinary
god, "wood of life," & he'll wince.

IV

Nuptial light in whitish bone: dense spikes

form the lady's crown. Hadesgreen—the shade, the toques—heron
feathers for my thigh

& three fangs placed in his jaw for luck. We wed again.
The calyx home, she says, & pry them off my eyelid.

v

I could pile my stones to sprout or
graft garden junk from the stalk to the fall of William. Devil break the red
hasp of your back. All raised untidy palms to sun—white &
         blades & laid limp curled around the grass. Hand that was his.
The seabirds pent into my cheeks.
Or I could pity

his buds carved
foxy on each kidney.   "Pearly everlastings."   Clap hands
& shoot inside his bulb, we pray.

I

He could be big. He could be sung by rocks.
A bloody sound. His head in sun. Really a throb
from my owling throat. Hanging.
Praise from stones.

William named my garden New York City. Then shoved me on my
knees. With the suckers, the fat flowers, which are
    the skirts of heavy walkers now bent
    in the garden. His women which are
    white ants which are termites which see.

II

Mismade him again. Mislaid him. A two-celled sac borne on the stalk
his hands behind his back. He grew profane
& big as a bottlefly. Bullfly. Covered
his left eye to wink at me. His thousand
hands grown from his ribbed-for-my-
pleasure side. He yanked us down with a bang.
Deny the gods of the garden, say. Their downy hands. Barang!

III

Love, tender as a beetle. It shoots down. It shoots
us down, pushing on the larynx. Pushed all our teeth back
and tongued the bark of our necks. Orchards of speech ax.

IV

He performed a miracle is right.

Hush! Hush! Shut your goddamn mouths he said.
To plant him in the city full of prayer is to
chain him to the bar.

Tender oyster-gut of eyelids, heal us.
William   his ear to the bar   healed. His little finger
extended back
          begat (begged) wax from the crowd.

V

Honey stop wrestling honey. I said I'd suckle for you. I said
I'd Sabbath and scatter the wafers for you. I sliced an orange
root to see the kids inside. God's kids.

Weak dirt. But the rain wills trees.

I

A cave with arms at the mouth.
Our hero is blind: everything he hears he sees.

Hear! Gold light sifts to his ear.
A roar. The seas
beaten—his duodenum, colon,
blind intestine and appendix, destined
for heat, they blush.

II

William's cabbage heart shook.
He dragged himself from the dirt.

If he could rest his ears he could see
ginkgos in his city. The pretty boy I mean
& Will, who were both aging
with their senses curbed until they knew
New York City by the root & crack.

III

As if there is a fig tree rooted in heaven
& each of its leaves knows all the rules.

8:45 a.m. hum: he saw the boy had fallen
into a manhole & the fig tree had fallen into a manhole
& neither could be the sound of hands splitting
gold hands landed
up the breadth of William's back.

      God bleeding me a kind of blooded cry
      my lady makes me a heron
      or my leg for a stump
      the cursed in loam my
      venomous thumbs my

His guts an a-readied muck.

IV

If your hand had been dusk-
yellow not a lantern but winged
—a bridge or a dove sprung
from the dirt.

Trying to make a shape. The feathered
thumb herring-
bone. We would not fall.

v

I brought you in from the garden since I can't
stand the trees' visions. William you will
be there the last
stately in ribbons.

But the vision is a fattened glee.
The glee is a clubfoot.
The glee is a mutt.
The eyes sewn up the air & nothing can be seen
but visions.

You are burst sideways like a fist in water.
Your maker staring into an apron of mud.
Thou art
        bore a hole in the man.
Thou art
        not a bloody bit, not the man.

Even the city hung open.
What innocence.
Giant buildings, streets and strips.
The sky met the roof but no resistance,
wind not felt through the heat.
Resolve, petal like a bag,
old tooth, plastic cup,
swept up.

And I, soldier, who am no longer maker but an eye
ran the river,
saw more or less the boy the trees,
what boy what trees   hung
against the lights.

REMEMBERING ANIMALS

I

You became left-handed,
exhausted, calling out a name.

2

Your face chitters scythe
once spirit has gone.

3

An imperial heart,
in a fanged city, it sings.
And sang alone.

4

Yet in the alert
warm animal—

here distance,
there breath.

5

I loosen, gently,
my work hair from the bun;
I release my
loose change from the skirt.

6

Waxwings, graphemes
fall, a portrait
tra-la translucent
gray ala dawn. We fa-la
fall as when. Along.

Having been given a name, let's say.
Bêtise. Our simple things have been
too simple altogether.
(As if man did not also receive his name
and names.)

The desert eye of God is missing and it's whole.
Dogs of the corpse. Corpse
of the face. Every living thing a hinge
and, at the heart of this, our analogy.

A shimmer in breeze picks us up, our scent a peal that calls us
outside rooms. *Ecce animot.* Unavoidable.

I see symptoms in words. I see the birds the trees the heavy grasses
been beaten,

his growl in the desert. I see Name of a dog. Name of a dog.

I intend an utterance.

This meatless a morning,
I laid the cherished dog in camp.
There was no doubt of man.

Dark dirt to make her cant into a bark.

A sticky scent responds a fatherland;
remakes a first son from the silt.

The son is a dog. The dog is a face and money talks.

The monkey talk of internment, machine that won't speak.

Lacking hostages, what can we shut up in sun, in morning?
An animal without response. Makes tracks.

A false start. Lovemaking—dansité—a lure to war. The hen-pigeon
pretends a capture—to leave a trace and track.

To wake in vital situations, in lawn and sky.
Isn't it obvious? What's done and not done to hunt

a warp in the root. We've found that cracked tomb,
gone down to reach the living creature. Ahuman, she's the one

to whom evil is foreign. Her cruel innocence infects.
My love a living danger wrought in sun. No tracks.

Only traces sweeping anterior to good
anterior to evil. Oh God oh man oh man a chill

that sun can't crease, our northern ball. The men in jeans.
The men in Yeats. The girl in boy. The boy on boy. The me front me.

Sky-burnt sea, beleaguered thing, wrapped in bandages of fog, we heal.
Our breast to the sand, we hear. Pigeons in the awning, rapture
in the offing—a sanding belt to skin. He's on screen, lowing.

Were our eyes to meet, thou shall not kill. Were we. To meet. Thou shall
not. Nothing like. Dying. Not having. Anything to do.

Cling to the men
to their song of wild bees
which is a song of her waist, spirit
out among splendor, song engraved
in what were waves.

It is no longer autumn

it is not yet spring
but a bright night.
Trees set ablaze in the west send up
a golden and fetid signal. *Animaux*.

1

On the wall, her series of red
dog paintings, all aerial views, leads
to the filthy bathroom she's shamed by
and bleaches until her hands run red.

2

Shame is a sudden thing.
A man tries to read
the dog that suffers
under cool lobby lights
as a sign.
seen and forgotten

3

Nothing robs us
of inherited furs.

Say, cat kingdom, lux gardens,
fingers inside a rabbit pocket
or mink.

4

When it comes to grief,
we don't agree
how best to keep
the rifle bolted
to the bed.

5

My shame
is ashamed of itself and calls me
stillness.

My heels dent the soft pine floor
within a life called animal.

6

Is it sad because it's mute?
I am not sad, mourning.

Announcing death,
I wear pearls.

My navy blue
is softer than black.

This one is called "Love of Her Shine,"

the hem of skirt
below or resting on the bed's edge.
Hands aim at the corner of the room.

Triangles unfold against the eye. The wealth of it
makes possible a meaning, we think.

You, who in navy skirt, in punched-out
shine, linked both her arms through mine.

Desert turns to road
where road becomes
that distant highway you thought
you might be remembering. Remembering
walking alongside ankles

in the driving rain.
We waded through
that which whites-out
that which is not coming.

As it receded, just the hem of it, halos
circled the deck chairs, the hotel pool
stung with rain.

Gulls swallow
the pads of your feet. That same fullness
which floats a summer skirt, floats the legs—
your limbs reflected in bands or to say

this is a second happiest nostalgia.
An absolute surface
of the sea   & our bodies
drink in the tinted light.

Print the deck with hands
& knees, begin
the splendid moment.

The heat imposes
possibility just before
the world loses principles.

Evaporates the empty spot.

I was to have
varied the shutter speeds,
soothing the mind.

I'm here to find out
how to leave with the self.

We'd been told she could be read by ear.
(The red side of a leaf.)
To burst through and leave only roots.

I can give you up and find
several years of the shape of
healthy living. Or I can build just this scene.

Loosen your limbs to be fed. Cross, we mean to say, into calm.
Summer winter autumn kept at bay. Roughly silvered leaves that are
the snow.
Love, take on a fuller luster!

I woke to the smell of apples like an open nerve, the scent a memory
pushed from sleep.

I have no and every reason to think you know and have closed
a devil into you. Holed gem. Hoping
that you'd spread
your praying fan on me.

What is wise could not repent in breath. In breath, repeats—
a ship,
curled groove that could this time end sea.

I

You live in a beautiful house.

2

You live in a beautiful house,
desperate to stay
where they felt your poverty.

And the ability of your house
to expose itself,

inside
or out.

3

If you turn out intimacy
without a space for
the singular, what will happen
happens in public. You won't see
gardens.

4

You live in a beautiful house
where love falls
over the sofa back,
        abashed, drunkenly.

5

I look inside your house at night.

If ever was a mirror
on the ceiling of hell,

it illuminates these
piled-together
bodies.

6

Shack, hovel, hut-life:
The knife by which you hand—

Love, leather smell stitched
in a circle to hold
the stub of knuckle
left open.

This is the way.

I

A boy was covered in pigeons.
He put birdseed in his hair and crotch so the ghostbird
would descend and devour him.

I saw the brown bird with the yellow breast
smoking Lucky Strikes. Thought she might be the Holy Spirit.
There are no birds only what this typewriter flushes out.
The cliffs are made from stone doves.
And the boys had beautiful lips.

II

The Outside suggests a tunnel to ride what he
says through a tunnel. Geography, animal life, the eventual
human being. Anatomy on the page
is sexier, my ghost.
The page of real thigh, my mister,
opens at the top to be eaten like
the sun you can recognize eats her rays. Greasy misery
covers my hands. It bothers
me to touch a carcass. Dead branches. Bothers me.

III

God's big eye is a pink cubicle.
God's big eye stretches
around me, a great balled gown.

I look for him in the roots of the roofless space.
Mons pubis corresponds to the real bird.

The lung. The wing.

IV

I demand the air beat. The birds scared
up into motion and I expect
revelation. I have my lusty knife.
Left cigarettes on your grave
and chant. J is for Jerusalem. Returns the poet to an invisible
homeland.
Resurrects the liver.
        Saying goodbye to a ghost is a hoax.
The birds are still in flight. Unhook the birds.

v

Sick orange sky I hate
I shall see it opened, the sunny aftertomb
and a real poem at the gate.

The erratic footprints of birds upon the sand or lacerations.
No limbs at our disposal, only the desire of limbs to reflesh.
The ghost gestures.

I am filling your borders with letters.
This is the new word—get up and live.

ACKNOWLEDGMENTS

Poems from this collection have appeared in *Action Yes, Can We Have Our Ball Back?*, *Greatcoat Magazine*, *Moria Poetry*, and *Sonora Review*; in the anthology *The Arcadia Project: The Postmodern Pastoral*, edited by Joshua Corey and G. C. Waldrep (Ahsahta Press, 2012); and in the chapbook *Ecce Animot* (Projective Industries, 2010).

Special thanks to my teachers and mentors for their wisdom and encouragement: James Galvin, Sara Langworthy, Julie Leonard, Mark Levine, Amy Margolis, Christopher Merrill, Dee Morris, Elizabeth Robinson, Mary Ruefle, Robyn Schiff, Robert Siegel, Eleni Sikelianos, Garrett Stewart, Cole Swensen, Marguerite Tassi, Nick Twemlow, Cathy Wagner, and Emily Wilson, and to my editor Janet Holmes for her wonderful guidance and keen editorial eye.

ABOUT THE AUTHOR

MARY HICKMAN was born in Idaho and grew up in China, Hong Kong, and Taiwan. She is a graduate of the Iowa Writers' Workshop where she received an Iowa Arts Fellowship. She works for the International Writing Program in Iowa City.

AHSAHTA PRESS

SAWTOOTH POETRY PRIZE SERIES

2002: Aaron McCollough, *Welkin* (Brenda Hillman, judge)

2003: Graham Foust, *Leave the Room to Itself* (Joe Wenderoth, judge)

2004: Noah Eli Gordon, *The Area of Sound Called the Subtone* (Claudia Rankine, judge)

2005: Karla Kelsey, *Knowledge, Forms, The Aviary* (Carolyn Forché, judge)

2006: Paige Ackerson-Kiely, *In No One's Land* (D. A. Powell, judge)

2007: Rusty Morrison, *the true keeps calm biding its story* (Peter Gizzi, judge)

2008: Barbara Maloutas, *the whole Marie* (C. D. Wright, judge)

2009: Julie Carr, *100 Notes on Violence* (Rae Armantrout, judge)

2010: James Meetze, *Dayglo* (Terrance Hayes, judge)

2011: Karen Rigby, *Chinoiserie* (Paul Hoover, judge)

2012: T. Zachary Cotler, *Sonnets to the Humans* (Heather McHugh, judge)

2013: David Bartone, *Practice on Mountains* (Dan Beachy-Quick, judge)

2014: Aaron Apps, *Dear Herculine* (Mei-mei Berssenbrugge, judge)

AHSAHTA PRESS

NEW SERIES

This book is set in Apollo MT type
with Titling Gothic FB Condensed titles
by Ahsahta Press at Boise State University.
Cover design by Quemadura.
Book design by Janet Holmes.

AHSAHTA PRESS
2015

JANET HOLMES, DIRECTOR
ADRIAN KIEN, ASSISTANT DIRECTOR

DENISE BICKFORD
KATIE FULLER
LAURA ROGHAAR
ELIZABETH SMITH
KERRI WEBSTER